The **Diabetic** Cookbook

delicious recipes to improve health and well-being

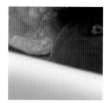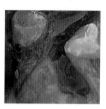

Love Food ® is an imprint of Parragon Books Ltd

Parragon
Queen Street House
4 Queen Street
Bath BA1 1HE, UK

Copyright © Parragon Books Ltd 2004

Love Food ® and the accompanying heart device is a trademark of Parragon Books Ltd

ISBN: 978-1-4075-3907-2

Printed in China

Designed and produced by THE BRIDGEWATER BOOK COMPANY
Cover Design: Andrew Easton at Ummgumma
Introduction, Nutritional Facts and Analysis: Charlotte Watt
Photography: Clive Bozzard-Hill
Home Economist: Phillipa Vanstone
Stylist: Angela Macfarlane

The publishers would like to thank the following companies for the loan of props: Dartington Crystal, Marlux Mills, Maxwell & Williams, Lifestyle Collections, Viners & Oneida, Typhoon and John Lewis.

NOTES FOR THE READER

This book uses imperial, metric, or US cup measurements. Follow the same units of measurement throughout; do not mix imperial and metric. All spoon measurements are level, unless otherwise stated: teaspoons are assumed to be 5 ml and tablespoons are assumed to be 15 ml.

Individual vegetables such as potatoes are medium and pepper is freshly ground black pepper. Milk used in the recipes is skim or semiskim to help limit the fat content of the meal. The recipes have been made with a reduced-fat and -sugar content in accordance with healthy eating guidelines. However, this means that they will not keep fresh for as long a period of time as their higher-fat and -sugar alternatives.

Some of the recipes require stock. If you use commercially made bouillon granules or cubes, these can have a relatively high salt content, so do not add any further salt. If you make your own stock, keep the fat and salt content to a minimum. Don't sauté the vegetables before simmering—just simmer the vegetables, herbs, and meat, poultry, or fish in water and strain. Meat and poultry stocks should be strained, cooled, and refrigerated before use so that the fat from the meat rises to the top and solidifies—it can then be easily removed and this reduces the saturated fat content of the meal. Homemade stocks should be stored in the refrigerator and used within two days, or frozen in usable portions and labeled.

Recipes using raw or very lightly cooked eggs should be avoided by infants, the elderly, pregnant women, convalescents, and anyone suffering from an illness.

Ovens should be preheated to the specified temperature. If using a fan-assisted oven, check the manufacturer's instructions for adjusting the time and temperature.

The values of the nutritional analysis for each recipe refer to a single serving, or a single slice where relevant. They do not include the serving suggestion. Where a range of portions is given the nutritional analysis figure refers to the mid-range figure. The calorific value given is in KCal (Kilocalories). The carbohydrate figure includes starches and sugars, with the sugar value then given separately. The fat figure is likewise the total fat, with the saturated part then given separately.

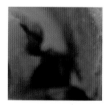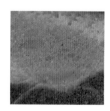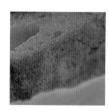

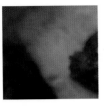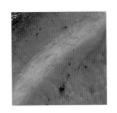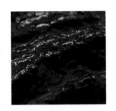

contents

Introduction

The diet that is most beneficial for a person with diabetes is actually healthy for anyone, especially if you want to reduce your risk of developing common conditions such as heart disease and stroke, high cholesterol, high blood pressure, and, of course, diabetes, if you have a family history of it. This book provides simple, sensible eating guidelines and recipes that will benefit all those with diabetes and the whole family besides, and offers a good starting point for establishing dietary awareness and taking control of your health. These dietary guidelines can also help you to manage your weight, in conjunction with a suitable exercise program and a controlled daily calorie intake. The recipes are also delicious, and the enjoyment of food is, after all, a very important factor. But this pleasure can be doubled if you know that what you are putting in your mouth is of benefit to your wellbeing and could significantly improve your quality of life.

The Nature of Diabetes

Diabetes is a condition characterized by an inability to produce the hormone insulin from the pancreas and therefore move glucose from the bloodstream into the cells and muscles where it is needed to produce energy. This causes an excess of sugar or glucose in the blood, which can lead to conditions associated with diabetes, such as obesity, heart disease, high cholesterol, and damage to nerves (neuropathies), eyes (retinopathy), and kidneys.

There are two types of diabetes:

Type I Diabetes is also called Insulin-Dependent Diabetes Mellitus (IDDM) and develops when the body stops producing insulin. This is due to the destruction of the cells in the pancreas that make insulin and it is believed to be a genetic condition. In most people it manifests before the age of 40 and must be controlled by injections and diet.

Type II Diabetes is also called Non-Insulin-Dependent Diabetes Mellitus (NIDDM), or adult-onset diabetes. This can occur as a result of a diet high in refined foods or sugars, where the pancreas has to produce so much insulin that it finally becomes exhausted and either produces less insulin or is unable to use the insulin that it does produce, leading to symptoms. This condition is also related to weight gain and a diet that helps control blood sugar is also effective for weight loss.

The same diet is advocated for both types of diabetes, but anyone would benefit from this dietary approach and the recipes in this book, as the main goals are to lose weight, protect the heart, and lower cholesterol to decrease the risk of associated conditions. For Type II, in some cases, if the diet is properly controlled and under medical supervision, this can help to reduce the amount of medication that needs to be taken.

Some people also suffer from a condition called **Syndrome X**, a potentially pre-diabetic state where the body becomes insensitive to insulin, and therefore cannot use it properly, leading to weight gain.

Symptoms of untreated diabetes include increased thirst, frequent urination with large volumes, fatigue, weight loss, skin and genital itching. If you have a combination of these and previous high sugar intake, see your doctor to check for diabetes. If you don't, these dietary guidelines could still help to relieve your symptoms, and if there is diabetes in your family, this diet can help to decrease your risk of developing it.

The Role of Nutrition in the Management of Diabetes

In relation to diabetes, "management" means to maintain near normal blood-sugar levels and increase the effectiveness of insulin in the body so that less is needed. This is called "increasing insulin sensitivity." As mentioned with Syndrome X (see box, left), people can be "insulin insensitive" and still produce insulin, so the following dietary advice will also be very helpful for them.

Insulin is normally released when sugar levels in the blood become higher than they should be. People with diabetes cannot reduce these blood-sugar levels without the aid of administered insulin. It was previously thought that this problem could be avoided by excluding carbohydrates entirely from the diet, but this has now been refuted. Carbohydrates are our main source of energy and should make up half our daily calorie intake. It is the kind of carbohydrates we eat and when that is crucial.

If you have Type I diabetes, the amount and timing of consumption of carbohydrates should be balanced with your dosage and timing of insulin medication. This needs to be discussed with your doctor.

If you have Type II diabetes, the relative lack of production of insulin should be considered and carbohydrate intake spread throughout the day. Again, this should be discussed with your doctor, especially if you are taking any medication.

The aim of the diet in this book is to keep blood-glucose levels as close to normal as possible, and this can be very simple and easy to achieve. A few basic changes to your diet that can make you feel better are very motivating. With blood-sugar control, when you eat is all-important; eating little and often maintains a slow, steady stream of glucose to the blood and a good breakfast sets the right levels for the day, meaning fewer cravings and more control over the food choices you make.

If blood-sugar levels are not properly controlled, damage can occur in the eyes, kidneys, heart, legs, and brain. This is why exercise is crucial; it helps blood-sugar control and increases circulation to these body parts, which helps to limit damage. Diet has also been shown to improve insulin sensitivity. This means that for those who produce some insulin, it can become more effective, and for those who produce none and need to medicate, they may find their levels easier to control. This also helps to limit the potential damage to arteries that high insulin levels have been shown to increase.

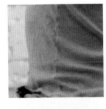

The Dietary Approach to Diabetes Management

As diabetes is heightened when blood-sugar levels become raised, the advice is to balance these levels by avoiding highs and lows. Sugar, salt, caffeine, alcohol, cigarettes, and refined and processed foods such as white bread, cakes, and pastries cause a rush of sugar into the bloodstream and should be avoided. After this initial surge, blood-sugar levels can then drop dramatically, even causing hypoglycemia, with symptoms such as sweating, hunger, anxiety, irritability, rapid heart rate, palpitations, blurred vision, tingling lips, and turning pale. Hypoglycemia can also be caused by too much medication (consult your doctor) or alcohol, which inhibits glucose production by the liver. To avoid these sudden dips in blood-sugar levels, try to keep them even by not missing meals and following the dietary advice given here. This can help stop imbalances that lead to vicious cycles, as foods that raise blood-sugar levels can create cravings for more of the same.

Many other conditions such as depression, headaches, fatigue, and insomnia are affected by fluctuating blood-sugar levels, and as they lead to high cholesterol and heart disease risk, this dietary advice is appropriate for everyone.

With diabetes, the balance of macronutrients—carbohydrates, fats, and proteins—is crucial. The National Institute of Diabetes and Digestive and Kidney Diseases (NIDDK) and The World Health Organization (WHO) recommend a diet high in complex carbohydrates, low in saturated fat, and high in fiber. This is because it is the combination of saturated fat and sugar that causes the accumulation of fat which increases insulin insensitivity, diabetes symptoms, risks, and side effects.

Carbohydrates

Carbohydrates, found in vegetables, fruit, cereal grains, and dairy products, are made from simple sugars, which all eventually break down to glucose. While carbohydrates are our main source of fuel and should make up half of our daily calorie intake, it is vital to make the right choice of the type of carbohydrate to be eaten, depending on the speed in which it breaks down into the glucose components in the body.

Refined carbohydrates or sugars are very simple molecules. What we call "sugar" for cooking and eating is actually sucrose—just two molecules of glucose that offer a very quick supply of sugar to the bloodstream, demanding a high need for insulin that the diabetic cannot supply. Sucrose is found in processed foods, candies, cakes, soft drinks, fruit juices, and very refined carbohydrates such as white bread, where the bran part of the wheat has been stripped away. This quick release of sugar can be laid down as fat if the body cannot employ insulin to use it correctly. Current research has shown that many diabetics may be eating more sugar than they think, because many have a reduced ability to taste sugar. Bringing down high blood-sugar levels is a priority; converting sugars into fat takes place in the liver and can lead to the obesity that is often associated with diabetes.

Complex carbohydrates, known as starches, release their sugars more slowly, so are used for energy rather than laid down as fat. These are termed starches. They also contain fiber, which also helps to slow down sugar release and eliminate toxins from the body to help prevent disease. The whole-grain bran part of cereal grains that is removed in white flour and processed foods contains fiber and provides glucose molecules that are bound together in more complex structures. Vegetables and fruit in their natural, raw state provide complex carbohydrates bound in fiber. They therefore take much more time to break down into their simple sugars and provide a more slow and steady release into the bloodstream, which is much easier for someone with little insulin to deal with. Pasta, potatoes, brown rice, and brown bread can be eaten in a diabetic diet if the appropriate fat-intake guidelines are also observed and they are eaten with proteins to slow down their release of sugars. The carbohydrate issue is, however, not as simple as previously thought—see the Glycemic Index (pages 10–11).

Fiber

Fiber can either be soluble or insoluble and a balance of both in the diet is very important for health in those with diabetes. Fiber helps to level out blood sugar by slowing down digestion and the release of sugar from food. Aim for 35 grams per day to balance blood sugar, lower cholesterol levels, clean the colon of toxins, and to help prevent heart disease.

Soluble fiber tends to be found in fruit and vegetables, such as apples, citrus fruits, carrots, cherries, avocados, beet, dried apricots and prunes, and also some seed husks such as linseed, oat bran, and psyllium husks, which many people take to counter constipation. It helps digestion by absorbing water and softening stools, and this can help lower cholesterol.

Insoluble fiber remains undigested and so clears the digestive system, prevents constipation, lessens the incidence of colon and rectal cancer, and speeds up the elimination of waste from the body. It is found in brown rice (the fiber is removed when processed to white), rye bread and crackers, lentils, asparagus, Brussels sprouts, cabbage, other whole-grains, and fibrous vegetables.

Oats are a complex carbohydrate, none of which turns directly into sugar in the body. They provide 10 percent of their weight in fiber and are a perfect breakfast food. Vegetables and fruit contain cellulose, an insoluble plant fiber that contains little sugar, but it is important to remember that when cooked these become broken down more readily into sugars. This is why vegetables such as carrots, bell peppers, and parsnips taste sweeter the longer they are cooked.

Fats

The stipulation of a high-carbohydrate, lowfat diet for diabetics does not mean that all fats should be avoided. Instead, it is a matter of choosing the right fats and consuming them in moderation. Lowering your intake of refined carbohydrates that cause the accumulation of body fat is a big factor, and including a controlled amount of beneficial oils and essential fats in your diet can lower cholesterol and help blood-sugar regulation.

Saturated fats tend to be from animal sources, such as butter and meat fats. They are solid at room temperature and can form in the same way in the body—if eaten in high amounts they can clog arteries and add to the risk of heart disease. In combination with sugars, they can become laid down as fat, and so foods combining both, such as pastries, are the main culprits of weight gain.

Monounsaturated oils are vegetable in origin and those traditionally eaten in Mediterranean countries, namely olive, almond, hazelnut, peanut, and avocado oils. They contain a fatty acid called oleic acid or omega-9 and remain liquid at room temperature, but begin to solidify when refrigerated. These have been found to have a neutral effect on blood cholesterol, although an excess can raise fat levels in the blood. The exception is olive oil, which has been shown actually to reduce blood cholesterol. However, this effect is thought to be caused by unique active components rather than the monounsaturated fat content. These are less damaged by heat than oils that stay liquid when chilled and therefore can be used for cooking.

Polyunsaturated fatty acids are always liquid and contain the essential fatty acids, the omega-6 oils, that help to produce localized hormones in the body, which are important for blood-sugar regulation. These include sesame, soy, walnut, pumpkin, and hemp oils. They are termed "essential" because they are crucial to body functions and must be consumed as they cannot be made in the body. Saturated fats can actually stop essential fats being used at a cellular level.

In the case of both polyunsaturated and monounsaturated fats, eating the nuts, seeds, and vegetables from which these oils are produced can also play a vital role in the effective management of diabetes. For example, the American Diabetes Association classes avocados as a "superfood" for diabetics, since not only do they contain beneficial oils but they also contain many nutrients that are important for cholesterol management and the protection of arteries against damage. Plant sterols (sterols are types of fat) help to reduce bad cholesterol and lutein helps to protect the eyes against diabetes-related degeneration. Although avocados, olives, nuts, and seeds also contain some saturated fats and should be eaten in moderation, they provide omega-6 oils, vitamin E, vitamins B_3 and B_6, zinc, and magnesium, which all aid blood-sugar management.

Omega-3 oils are those found in oily fish such as salmon, tuna, herring, mackerel, trout, and sardines. Like the omega-6 oils, these are essential fatty acids and are crucial to our health. Much research has shown how important these are for heart health; they should be eaten 3–4 times a week, in variety. Both omega-3 and omega-6 oils protect parts of the body that are rich in fats, and these areas of the body may commonly become damaged in a person with diabetes—the eyes, kidneys, liver, and circulation from the heart. For vegetarians, hemp, pumpkin, soy, and walnut oils contain some omega-3 oils but are higher in omega-6. Omega-3 and omega-6 should be eaten in a one-to-one ratio and flax or linseed can be added to food as a source of omega-3 oils.

Proteins

Proteins are the major source of building materials for the body. They can also be used as a source of energy that is released very slowly. They are therefore very good for blood-sugar management and can slow down sugar release into the bloodstream if eaten with less complex carbohydrates. Caution should be taken not to obtain these only from high-fat sources such as meats, but also from eggs, lowfat dairy products, and vegetable sources such as beans, and in small amounts from other vegetables such as broccoli and cauliflower.

The Glycemic Index (GI)

Research into sugars and their release into the bloodstream has found that some foods behave in a surprising way when introduced into the body. It is no longer enough just to distinguish between simple sugars and complex carbohydrates in the diabetic kitchen. As we are unable to predict how a food will act by its sugar and starch content alone, a table called the Glycemic Index has been drawn up to compare the release of sugar into the bloodstream that foods create against a measure of 100 for glucose. In the table, foods are categorized into high, medium, and low. High (more than 70) means that sugars are released very quickly, near to the speed of glucose itself. These foods should not be eaten on their own or they can cause a quick increase of blood sugar. They can, however, be eaten in small amounts at the same time as a food with a low score (under 55). This would equal a combined score in the medium range (55–70) and a good control of blood sugar. You should aim to include as many foods in the low range as possible for the best blood-sugar control and include those in the medium or high categories only with protein or other low-GI foods.

A low-GI diet can help to increase the body's sensitivity to insulin so that the insulin you do have works more effectively and less damage is likely to occur to nerves. It can also help to keep blood fats low, in conjunction with a low-saturated fat diet, and therefore reduce heart disease-related risks.

Certain foods shown in the table may surprise you in terms of release of sugars—corn flakes and parsnips, for instance, have very high scores and should be eaten with foods that bring the score down overall. Proteins and oils are not included in the Glycemic Index as they are known to be low-GI foods since they do not contain carbohydrates. Therefore, they can be eaten with the high-GI foods to slow down sugar release, for instance lean chicken with parsnips and low-GI nuts with corn flakes.

Low-GI Foods—below 55

Fruit and Fruit Juices

Cherries	22
Grapefruit	25
Dried apricots	31
Pears	37
Apples	38
Plums	39
Apple juice	41
Peaches	42
Oranges	44
Grapes	46
Pineapple juice	46
Grapefruit juice	48
Orange juice	52
Kiwifruit	53
Banana	54

Vegetables

Broccoli	10
Cabbage	10
Lettuce	10
Mushrooms	10
Raw onions	10
Raw red bell peppers	10
Raw carrots	49
Sweet potatoes	54

Grains

Pearl barley	31
Rye	34
Brown basmati rice	52

Breads

Mixed grain bread	48
Pumpernickel rye bread	50

Pasta

Vermicelli	35
Linguine	42
Instant noodles	47

Bakery Products

Sponge cake (made with egg)	46

Breakfast Cereals

Bran cereal	42

Dairy

Lowfat yogurt	14
Whole milk	27
Skim milk	27
Lowfat fruit yogurt	33
Custard	43

Legumes

Soybeans	14
Red split lentils	18
Green lentils	29
Canned chickpeas	42
Canned pinto beans	45
Green peas	48

Medium-GI Foods—55–70

Fruit and Fruit Juices

Mangoes	56
Golden raisins	56
Apricots	57
Raisins	64
Pineapple	66

Vegetables

Corn	55
New potatoes	57
Beet	64
Boiled or mashed potatoes	70

Grains

Brown rice	55
Buckwheat	55
White basmati rice	58

Breads

White pita bread	58
Hamburger bun	61
Rye flour bread	64
High-fiber wheat bread	68
Whole-wheat bread	69

Pasta

Durum wheat spaghetti	55

Bakery Products

Pastry	59
Muffins	62
Croissant	67

Breakfast Cereals

Granola	56
Porridge	61
Spun wheat cookie	69
Wheat biscuits	70

Cookies

Oatmeal cookies	55
Digestive cookies	59
Shortbread	64

Savory Cookies

Wheat thins	67

Dairy

Ice cream	61

Sugars

High-fruit jelly	55
Honey	58
Table sugar	64

Candies and Snacks

Popcorn	55

Beverages

Orange cordial	66
Orange soda	68

High-GI Foods—above 70

Vegetables

Rutabaga	72
French fries	75
Pumpkin	75
Baked potatoes	85
Cooked carrots	85
Parsnips	97

Legumes

Fava beans	79

Grains

White rice	88

Breads

White bagel	72
White wheat bread	78
Gluten-free bread	90
French baguette	95

Bakery Products

Doughnuts	76
Waffles	76

Breakfast Cereals

Wheat bran flakes with added dried fruit	71
Puffed wheat	74
Crisped rice	82
Corn flakes	83

Savory Cookies and Crackers

Water biscuits	71
Rice cakes	77

Candies and Snacks

Corn tortillas	74
Jelly beans	80
Pretzels	81
Dates	99

Beverages

High-glucose sports drinks	95

This approach has been used in the book to create low- and medium-GI recipes that might still contain high-GI foods but do not raise blood-sugar levels beyond the 'normal' range by combining for average scores. You will see from the table that some 'treat' foods such as ice cream and cookies have surprisingly low GI scores, but this is often due to their high fat content and they should still be eaten sparingly.

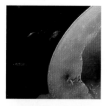

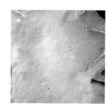

General Dietary Advice

For people with diabetes, the emphasis should be on consuming as much raw fruit and vegetables and fresh vegetable juices as possible where practical. This ensures a slow release of sugar into the bloodstream and the intake of as much insoluble fiber and the most nutrient-dense foods as possible.

The mineral chromium helps make a substance called Glucose Tolerance Factor (GTF) in the body, and aids the function of insulin and consequently the uptake of sugar by cells. This is therefore of particular importance to people with diabetes and may help those with Type II to increase insulin sensitivity. It is found in whole-wheat bread, rye bread, potatoes, green bell peppers, eggs, chicken, and apples.

Foods that contain nutrients needed for blood-sugar balance (zinc, magnesium, vitamins B_3, B_6, and C) are nuts, seeds, fish, dark green vegetables, brassicas (broccoli, cabbage, cauliflower, kale), beans, peas, eggs, avocados, oats, red/yellow/orange fruit, onions, and asparagus. These foods are also important for managing cholesterol levels and lowering the risk of heart disease—which are important considerations for people with diabetes.

Avoiding stimulants (caffeine, alcohol, and cigarettes) helps to eliminate the "highs and lows" of blood sugar and reduce sugar cravings.

Reducing the Risk of Associated Conditions

Changing what and how you eat can reduce the risk of the diseases associated with diabetes such as neuropathies, kidney damage, and retinopathy. These can occur when excess sugars in the blood harden. High blood pressure is also a concern for diabetics, and although diet can play a part here, it is important to emphasize how exercise and weight management can increase the benefits of a good diet. Exercising little and often—even daily walking—can have a more profound effect on circulation and these conditions than short, intermittent bursts of activity.

Foods that increase circulation, such as dark and brightly colored vegetables (whose pigments contain beneficial plant chemicals) and sulfur foods such as onions, garlic, eggs, broccoli, fennel, and beans, are also good for blood-sugar control. Vitamin C foods, specifically Brussels sprouts, black currants, parsley, kale, savoy cabbage, broccoli, bell peppers, tomatoes, kiwifruit, orange juice, mangoes, cauliflower, snow peas, peas, and sweet potatoes, help to prevent the incidence of secondary conditions and protect the body from damage. All the aforementioned foods also contain different vitamins and plant chemicals, especially carotenoids which protect fatty areas of the body that tend to get damaged in people with diabetes—the eyes, kidneys, liver, and circulation from the heart.

It must also be pointed out that people with diabetes who smoke are two to three times more likely to develop kidney damage, according to research carried out at Colorado University Health Sciences Center, because smoking constricts the blood vessels.

About the Recipes

When putting together the recipes in this book, practicality and ease were important factors. Choices were made to provide you with an accessible diet and versions of familiar recipes more beneficial to someone with diabetes. The overall GI score of combinations of foods was considered and a rating of either low or medium has been assigned to each recipe. It makes sense for you to prioritize those that are low and eat the medium ones less often. It is also important to vary your diet and the recipes to ensure a good spread of carbohydrates, fats, and proteins. Check the nutritional information accompanying each recipe to help you obtain an overall diet that is low in fat and sugar and high in complex carbohydrates. When choosing recipes for one day, for instance, consider the balance of these macronutrients and try to obtain half of your daily calorie intake from carbohydrates, including snacks such as fruit.

A nutritional fact is also provided for each recipe which highlights the specific health benefits of certain foods for those with diabetes, for instance in balancing blood sugar, increasing the uptake of insulin, encouraging circulation to lower the risk of nerve damage, cleansing the body, lowering blood pressure and cholesterol levels, and protecting against eye and kidney damage. Foods that are said to be of particular benefit to people with diabetes are blueberries, cinnamon, chicory, onion, beans, garlic, olive oil, nuts, and avocados. These should be included in your diet often, but remember that a variety of foods is paramount to health, to ensure a full range and balance of nutrients.

The choice of specific varieties of ingredients used in the recipes also takes into account their effect on the release of blood sugar. For instance, if rice is featured in a recipe, brown basmati has been chosen as the best option. In the same way, consideration has been given to the choice of oils and types of fiber and carbohydrates, and this is reflected in the nutritional breakdowns.

Breakfasts & Brunches

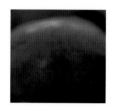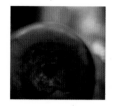

This chapter offers a selection of sweet and savory dishes that should satisfy a healthy appetite while still being well balanced and delicious. All the dishes can be prepared relatively quickly. For a brunch party, you can think about offering a selection; for instance the Bircher Granola or Yogurt with Honey, Nuts & Blueberries, followed by Mexican Eggs, and accompanied by Honey & Lemon Muffins.

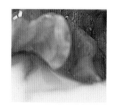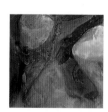

serves 4

Baked Eggs with Spinach

Ingredients

1 tbsp olive oil

3 shallots, finely chopped

1 lb 2 oz/500 g baby spinach leaves

4 tbsp light cream

freshly grated nutmeg

pepper

4 large eggs

4 tbsp Parmesan cheese, finely grated

toasted whole-wheat bread, to serve

Nutritional Fact
Eggs contain lecithin, which helps to break down fats in the liver and improves sugar metabolism.

Serving Analysis
- *Calories*   185
- *Protein*   12g
- *Carbohydrate*   6.3g
- *Sugars*   1g
- *Fat*   13.3g
- *Saturates*   4.4g
- *GI*   Low

1 Preheat the oven to 400°F/200°C. Heat the oil in a skillet over medium heat, add the shallots, and cook, stirring frequently, for 4–5 minutes, or until soft. Add the spinach, cover, and cook for 2–3 minutes, or until the spinach has wilted. Remove the lid and cook until all the liquid has evaporated.

2 Add the cream to the spinach and season to taste with nutmeg and pepper. Spread the spinach mixture over the base of a shallow gratin dish and make 4 wells in the mixture with the back of a spoon.

3 Crack an egg into each well and sprinkle over the cheese. Bake in the preheated oven for 12–15 minutes, or until the eggs are set. Serve with whole-wheat toast.

makes 12

Honey & Lemon Muffins

Ingredients

$1/4$ cup unrefined superfine sugar

2 tbsp unsalted butter, melted and cooled slightly

$2/3$ cup buttermilk

2 eggs, beaten

4 tbsp flower honey

finely grated rind of 1 lemon and juice of $1/2$ lemon

scant $1^5/8$ cups all-purpose flour

$2^3/4$ cups oat bran

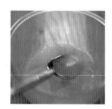

$1^1/2$ tbsp baking powder

Nutritional Fact

Honey is just 58 on the Glycemic Index, meaning it can be used very sparingly to sweeten foods.

Serving Analysis

• Calories	165
• Protein	5.7g
• Carbohydrate	33g
• Sugars	10.8g
• Fat	3.7g
• Saturates	1.6g
• GI	Medium

1 Preheat the oven to 350°F/180°C. Line a 12-hole muffin pan with muffin paper cases.

2 Put the sugar into a pitcher and add the butter, buttermilk, eggs, half the honey, and lemon rind. Mix briefly to combine.

3 Sift the flour into a large mixing bowl, add the oat bran and baking powder, and stir to combine. Make a well in the center of the flour mixture and add the buttermilk mixture. Quickly mix together—do not overmix; the batter should be slightly lumpy.

4 Spoon the batter into the paper cases and bake in the preheated oven for 25 minutes. Turn out onto a wire rack.

5 Mix the lemon juice with the remaining honey in a small bowl or pitcher and drizzle over the muffins while they are still hot. Let the muffins stand for 10 minutes before serving.

serves 4

Yogurt with Honey, Nuts & Blueberries

Nutritional Fact

Excellent for balancing blood sugar, blueberries are, therefore, a good food with which to start the day.

Serving Analysis
- *Calories* — *239*
- *Protein* — *4.3g*
- *Carbohydrate* — *24g*
- *Sugars* — *19.4g*
- *Fat* — *15.6g*
- *Saturates* — *2.7g*
- *GI* — *Low*

1 Heat the honey in a small pan over medium heat, add the nuts and stir until they are well coated. Remove from the heat and let cool slightly.

2 Divide the yogurt between 4 serving bowls, then spoon over the nut mixture and blueberries.

Ingredients

3 tbsp honey

generous ⅝ cup mixed unsalted nuts

8 tbsp plain yogurt

⅞ cup fresh blueberries

serves 4

Spicy Eggs

Nutritional Fact
A good protein breakfast helps to sustain good blood-sugar levels throughout the day.

Serving Analysis
- *Calories*   279
- *Protein*   15.8g
- *Carbohydrate*   4.9g
- *Sugars*   3.9g
- *Fat*   21.8g
- *Saturates*   6.3g
- *GI*   Low

1 Beat the eggs, milk, and pepper to taste in a large bowl. Set aside.

2 Heat the oil in a nonstick skillet over medium heat, add the red bell pepper and chili and cook, stirring frequently, for 5 minutes, or until the red bell pepper is soft and browned in places. Add the chorizo and cook until just browned. Transfer to a warmed plate and set aside.

3 Return the skillet to the heat, add the egg mixture, and cook to a soft scramble. Add the chorizo mixture, stir to combine and sprinkle over the cilantro. Serve at once on toasted whole-wheat bread.

Ingredients

8 large eggs

2 tbsp milk

pepper

1 tsp olive oil

1 red bell pepper, seeded and thinly sliced

1/2 fresh red chili

1 fresh chorizo sausage, skinned and sliced

4 tbsp chopped fresh cilantro

4 slices toasted whole-wheat bread, to serve

serves 4

Baked Mushrooms

Ingredients

2 tbsp olive oil

8 portobello mushrooms

2 oz/55 g white mushrooms, finely chopped

2 garlic cloves, crushed

4 slices lean cooked ham, finely chopped

2 tbsp finely chopped fresh parsley

pepper

4 slices rye bread, to serve

Nutritional Fact
Parsley is a good stress tonic that helps to keep blood-sugar levels manageable.

Serving Analysis
- Calories   124
- Protein   6.6g
- Carbohydrate   4g
- Sugars   1.2g
- Fat   9.7g
- Saturates   0.8g
- GI   Low

1 Preheat the oven to 375°F/190°C. Brush a baking sheet with a little of the oil. Arrange the portobello mushrooms, cup-side up, on the baking sheet.

2 Mix the white mushrooms, garlic, ham, and parsley together in a bowl.

3 Divide the ham mixture between the portobello mushroom cups. Drizzle with the remaining oil and season to taste with pepper.

4 Bake in the preheated oven for 10 minutes, then serve at once with rye bread.

serves 4

Onion & Gruyère Frittata

Ingredients

1 tbsp olive oil
1 garlic clove, crushed
2 red onions, thinly sliced
8 eggs
3¹/₂ oz/100 g Gruyère cheese, grated
pepper
4 slices soda bread, to serve

1 Heat the oil in a nonstick skillet over medium–low heat, add the garlic and onions, and cook, stirring occasionally, for 10 minutes, or until the onions are very soft and a little caramelized.

2 Beat the eggs with half the cheese and pepper to taste in a large bowl, pour over the onions, and gently stir until the eggs are evenly distributed. Cook for 5 minutes, or until the eggs are set on the bottom.

3 Meanwhile, preheat the broiler to high. Sprinkle the remaining cheese over the frittata and place under the preheated broiler until the cheese is melted. Cut the frittata into 4 wedges and serve at once with soda bread.

Nutritional Fact
Onions contain sulfur, which is good for the circulation and liver. Both are important for people with diabetes.

Serving Analysis
- *Calories*   304
- *Protein*   20.6g
- *Carbohydrate*   6.3g
- *Sugars*   2.9g
- *Fat*   21.7g
- *Saturates*   7.9g
- *GI*   Low

serves 4

Bircher Granola

Ingredients

scant 1 3/4 cups rolled oats

1 cup apple juice

1 apple, grated

1/2 cup plain yogurt

scant 3/4 cup blackberries

2 plums, pitted and sliced

2 tbsp honey

Nutritional Fact

Oats release their sugars very slowly, making them a good breakfast food.

Serving Analysis

• Calories	285
• Protein	8.4g
• Carbohydrate	56g
• Sugars	25.5g
• Fat	4.2g
• Saturates	1.1g
• GI	Low

1 Put the oats and apple juice into a mixing bowl and combine well. Cover and let chill overnight.

2 To serve, stir the apple and yogurt into the soaked oats and divide between 4 serving bowls. Top with the blackberries and plums and drizzle with the honey.

serves 4

Asparagus with Poached Eggs & Parmesan

Ingredients

10¹/₂ oz/300 g asparagus, trimmed

4 large eggs

3 oz/85 g Parmesan cheese

pepper

Nutritional Fact

Asparagus is known to be beneficial to the kidneys, which can be damaged if a person has diabetes.

Serving Analysis

* Calories   175
* Protein   15.6g
* Carbohydrate   4.7g
* Sugars   1.8g
* Fat   10.6g
* Saturates   5g
* GI   Low

1 Bring 2 pans of water to a boil. Add the asparagus to 1 pan, return to a simmer, and cook for 5 minutes, or until just tender.

2 Meanwhile, reduce the heat of the second pan to a simmer and carefully crack in the eggs, one at a time. Poach for 3 minutes, or until the whites are just set but the yolks are still soft. Remove with a slotted spoon.

3 Drain the asparagus and divide between 4 warmed plates. Top each plate of asparagus with an egg and shave over the cheese. Season to taste with pepper and serve at once.

Soups & Light Meals

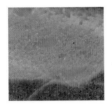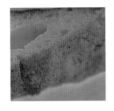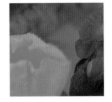

Eating a healthy diet doesn't mean sacrificing taste and
variety, and the recipes in this chapter illustrate how to use
ingredients and influences from around the world to produce
sophisticated and tasty light dishes. These recipes are flexible
since they can almost all be eaten as first courses for a dinner
party as well as light lunches on their own. The Crab Cakes
and Coconut Shrimp would also make good party offerings.

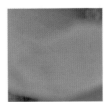

serves 4

Soup au Pistou

Ingredients

4 cups fresh cold water

bouquet garni of 1 fresh parsley sprig, 1 fresh thyme sprig, and 1 bay leaf, tied together with clean string

2 celery stalks, chopped

3 baby leeks, chopped

4 baby carrots, chopped

5 1/2 oz/150 g new potatoes, scrubbed and cut into bite-size chunks

4 tbsp shelled fava beans or peas

6 oz/175 g canned cannellini or flageolet beans, drained and rinsed

3 heads bok choy

scant 3 3/8 cups arugula

pepper

For the pistou

2 large handfuls fresh basil leaves

1 fresh green chili, seeded

2 garlic cloves

4 tbsp olive oil

1 tsp Parmesan cheese, finely grated

1 Put the water and bouquet garni into a large pan and add the celery, leeks, carrots, and potatoes. Bring to a boil, then reduce the heat and let simmer for 10 minutes.

2 Stir in the fava beans or peas and canned beans and let simmer for an additional 10 minutes. Stir in the bok choy, arugula, and pepper to taste and let simmer for an additional 2–3 minutes. Remove and discard the bouquet garni.

3 Meanwhile, to make the pistou, put the basil, chili, garlic, and oil into a food processor and pulse to form a thick paste. Stir in the cheese.

4 Stir most of the pistou into the soup, then ladle into warmed bowls. Top with the remaining pistou and serve at once.

Nutritional Fact
Beans contain soluble fiber. This balances blood sugar and cleanses the body.

Serving Analysis

• Calories	370
• Protein	19g
• Carbohydrate	46g
• Sugars	13.3g
• Fat	17g
• Saturates	0.6g
• GI	Medium

serves 4

Chicken with Linguine & Artichokes

Ingredients

4 chicken breasts, skinned

finely grated rind and juice of 1 lemon

2 tbsp olive oil

2 garlic cloves, crushed

14 oz/400 g canned artichoke hearts, drained and sliced

9 oz/250 g baby plum tomatoes

10½ oz/300 g dried linguine

To serve

chopped fresh parsley

Parmesan cheese, finely grated

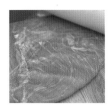

Nutritional Fact
Artichokes contain cynarin, which helps lower cholesterol. Cholesterol levels can rise when blood-sugar levels fluctuate.

Serving Analysis

• Calories	534
• Protein	41g
• Carbohydrate	66g
• Sugars	2.9g
• Fat	10g
• Saturates	0.03g
• GI	Medium

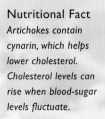

1 Put each chicken breast in turn between 2 pieces of plastic wrap and bash with a rolling pin to flatten. Put the chicken into a shallow, nonmetallic dish with the lemon rind and juice and 1 tablespoon of the oil and turn to coat in the marinade. Cover and let marinate in the refrigerator for 30 minutes.

2 Put a large pan of water on to boil. Heat the remaining oil in a skillet over low heat, add the garlic, and cook for 1 minute, stirring frequently. Add the artichokes and tomatoes and cook for 5 minutes, stirring occasionally. Add about half the marinade from the chicken and cook over medium heat for an additional 5 minutes.

3 Meanwhile, preheat the broiler to high. Remove the chicken from the remaining marinade and arrange on the broiler pan. Cook the chicken under the preheated broiler for 5 minutes each side until thoroughly cooked through. Meanwhile, add the linguine to the boiling water and cook for 7–9 minutes, or until just tender.

4 Drain the pasta and return to the pan, pour over the artichoke and tomato mixture, and slice in the cooked chicken.

5 Divide between 4 warmed plates and sprinkle over the parsley and cheese.

serves 4

Hot-&-Sour Soup with Tofu

Nutritional Fact
Ginger and garlic are good for the circulation, and vegetable protein is a better choice than meat protein for a diet with a low saturated-fat content.

Serving Analysis

• *Calories*	*353*
• *Protein*	*17g*
• *Carbohydrate*	*44g*
• *Sugars*	*2.7g*
• *Fat*	*12.8g*
• *Saturates*	*2g*
• *GI*	*Low*

Ingredients

3 strips of rind and juice of 1 lime

2 garlic cloves, peeled

2 slices fresh gingerroot

4 cups low-salt chicken stock

1 tbsp vegetable oil

5¹/₂ oz/150 g firm tofu (drained weight), cubed

7 oz/200 g dried fine egg noodles

3¹/₂ oz/100 g shiitake mushrooms, sliced

1 fresh red chili, seeded and sliced

4 scallions, sliced

1 tsp low-salt soy sauce

1 tsp Chinese rice wine

1 tsp sesame oil

chopped fresh cilantro, to garnish

1 Put the lime rind, garlic, and ginger into a large pan with the stock and bring to a boil. Reduce the heat and let simmer for 5 minutes. Remove the lime rind, garlic, and ginger with a slotted spoon and discard.

2 Meanwhile, heat the vegetable oil in a large skillet over high heat, add the tofu, and cook, turning frequently, until golden. Remove from the skillet and drain on paper towels.

3 Add the noodles, mushrooms, and chili to the stock and let simmer for 3 minutes. Add the tofu, scallions, soy sauce, lime juice, rice wine, and sesame oil and briefly heat through.

4 Divide the soup between 4 warmed bowls, sprinkle over the cilantro, and serve at once.

makes 12

Crab Cakes with Dipping Sauce

Ingredients

For the crab cakes

4 scallions

$10^{1}/_{2}$ oz/300 g raw shrimp, shelled and deveined

$10^{1}/_{2}$ oz/300 g cooked white crabmeat

1 tsp finely chopped capers

2 tsp chopped fresh dill

white pepper

1 small egg, lightly beaten

1 tsp Dijon mustard

1 tbsp all-purpose flour, plus extra for flouring

vegetable oil, for pan-frying

For the dipping sauce

2 tbsp finely chopped fresh gingerroot

6 tbsp low-salt soy sauce

3 tbsp honey

juice of 1 lime

2 tbsp sesame oil

Nutritional Fact

Fish is packed with protein, but low in saturated fat. It helps stabilize blood-sugar levels and protect against stress. All the sugar here is in the dip; each crab cake is practically sugar-free.

Serving Analysis

- Calories   111
- Protein   11.4g
- Carbohydrate   6.6g
- Sugars   4.7g
- Fat   4.5g
- Saturates   0.7g
- GI   Low

1 First make the dipping sauce. Put the ginger, soy sauce, and honey into a small pan and let simmer for 3 minutes. Remove from the heat and stir in the lime juice and sesame oil. Set aside. Transfer to a small serving dish when cool.

2 Put the scallions into a food processor and pulse to chop finely. Add the shrimp, crabmeat, and capers and process to combine. Turn into a bowl and mix in the dill, pepper to taste, egg, mustard, and flour.

3 With floured hands, shape the mixture into 12 cakes and put on a large plate. Cover and let chill in the refrigerator for 1 hour.

4 Heat a little vegetable oil in a large skillet over medium heat. Cook the crab cakes, in batches, for 3–4 minutes on each side. Remove from the skillet with a slotted spoon and drain on paper towels. Keep the crab cakes hot while cooking the remainder.

5 Serve the crab cakes hot with the dipping sauce.

serves 4

Trout Fillets with Lime, Sesame & Chili

Ingredients

2 tbsp sesame seeds

scant 1 1/4 cups fish stock

8 trout fillets, about 5 1/2 oz/150 g each

9 oz/250 g dried fine egg noodles

juice of 1/2 lime

1 fresh red chili, seeded and thinly sliced

1 tbsp sesame oil, plus extra for drizzling

1 tbsp vegetable oil

1 tsp Thai fish sauce

To serve

1 bunch watercress

4 lime wedges

Nutritional Fact
Trout contains good levels of essential fatty acids. These are the good fats that can help stabilize blood-sugar levels.

Serving Analysis

• Calories	563
• Protein	45g
• Carbohydrate	48g
• Sugars	1.4g
• Fat	19.5g
• Saturates	3.7g
• GI	Low

1 Heat a nonstick skillet over medium heat, add the sesame seeds, and cook, turning, until they start to color. Tip onto a plate and set aside.

2 Put the stock into a large skillet and bring to a simmer. Add the trout fillets and poach gently for 7–10 minutes, or until just cooked.

3 Meanwhile, bring a large pan of water to a boil, add the noodles, and cook for 3 minutes. Drain and toss with the sesame seeds, lime juice, chili, oils, and fish sauce. Keep warm.

4 To serve, pile an equal quantity of noodles on each of 4 serving plates and top with 2 trout fillets, some watercress, and a lime wedge. Drizzle with a little more sesame oil.

serves 4

Tuscan Bean Soup

Ingredients

1 tbsp olive oil

4 slices pancetta or thin-cut bacon slices, diced

2 garlic cloves, crushed

1 large red onion, thinly sliced

1 lb 12 oz/800 g canned cannellini beans, drained and rinsed

1 fresh rosemary sprig

4 cups low-salt chicken or vegetable stock

pepper

To garnish

olive oil

chopped fresh parsley

1 Heat the oil in a large pan over medium heat, add the pancetta, and cook for 1–2 minutes, stirring frequently. Add the garlic and onion and cook for 10 minutes, stirring occasionally, until the onion is soft and translucent.

2 Add the beans, rosemary, and stock and simmer over low heat for 15 minutes.

3 Remove and discard the rosemary. Let the soup cool slightly, then transfer, in small batches, to a food processor or blender and process until blended but not entirely smooth. Return to a clean pan and gently heat through. Season to taste with pepper.

4 Serve in warmed bowls drizzled with oil and sprinkled with parsley.

Nutritional Fact
Adding rosemary to cooking helps to prevent the damaging effects of heating fats.

Serving Analysis

• Calories	334
• Protein	24g
• Carbohydrate	40g
• Sugars	3.7g
• Fat	7.6g
• Saturates	1.2g
• GI	Low

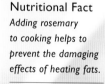

serves 4

Chicory & Walnut Salad with Goat Cheese & Pomegranate Seeds

Ingredients

14 oz/400 g chicory

scant 1 cup walnut pieces

seeds from 1 pomegranate

2 tbsp walnut oil

2 tsp red wine vinegar

1 tsp Dijon mustard

pepper

4 slices whole-wheat bread

2 garlic cloves, halved

4 x 3$\frac{1}{2}$-oz/100-g goat cheeses, with rind

3 tsp olive oil

Nutritional Fact

Chicory contains inulin, a natural fructose that helps people with diabetes to lower insulin levels.

Serving Analysis

• Calories	779
• Protein	33g
• Carbohydrate	29g
• Sugars	3.2g
• Fat	62g
• Saturates	24g
• GI	Low

1 Divide the heads of chicory into leaves and rinse, pat dry with paper towels, and arrange on 4 serving plates. Sprinkle over the walnut pieces and pomegranate seeds.

2 To make the dressing, whisk the walnut oil with the vinegar and mustard in a small bowl. Season with pepper and set aside.

3 Preheat the broiler to high. Rub the bread with the garlic. Arrange the goat cheeses on a sheet of foil and place on the broiler pan with the bread alongside. Cook under the preheated broiler until the bread is toasted on both sides and the cheese is bubbling.

4 To serve, drizzle each toasted bread slice with the olive oil, and top with a goat cheese. Put one goat cheese toast on each salad and drizzle the whole dish with the dressing.

serves 4

Coconut Shrimp with Cucumber Salad

1 Bring a large pan of water to a boil, add the rice, and cook for 25 minutes, or until tender. Drain and keep in a strainer covered with a clean dish towel to absorb the steam.

2 Meanwhile, soak 8 wooden skewers in cold water for 30 minutes, then drain.

3 Crush the coriander seeds in a mortar with a pestle. Heat a nonstick skillet over medium heat, add the crushed coriander seeds, and cook, turning, until they start to color. Tip onto a plate and set aside.

4 Put the egg whites into a shallow bowl and the coconut into a separate bowl. Roll each shrimp first in the egg whites, then in the coconut. Thread onto a skewer. Repeat so that each skewer is threaded with 3 coated shrimp.

5 Preheat the broiler to high. Using a potato peeler, peel long strips from the cucumber to create ribbons, put into a strainer to drain, then toss with the scallions and oil in a bowl, and set aside.

6 Cook the shrimp under the preheated broiler for 3–4 minutes on each side, or until pink and slightly browned.

7 Meanwhile, mix the rice with the toasted coriander seeds and fresh cilantro and press into 4 dariole molds or individual ramekins. Invert each mold onto a serving plate and divide the cucumber salad between the plates. Serve with the hot shrimp skewers, garnished with lime wedges.

Ingredients

1 cup brown basmati rice
$\frac{1}{2}$ tsp coriander seeds
2 egg whites, lightly beaten
generous $\frac{3}{4}$ cup dry unsweetened coconut
24 raw jumbo shrimp, shelled and tails left intact
$\frac{1}{2}$ cucumber
4 scallions, thinly sliced lengthwise
1 tsp sesame oil
1 tbsp finely chopped fresh cilantro
1 lime, cut into wedges, to garnish

Nutritional Fact
Brown basmati rice is a great stabilizer of blood-sugar levels and helps to keep down sugar cravings.

Serving Analysis

• Calories	412
• Protein	16g
• Carbohydrate	47g
• Sugars	3.1g
• Fat	19g
• Saturates	14.6g
• GI	Low

Seafood, Meat & Poultry

 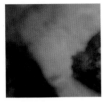   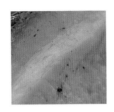 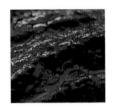

This chapter offers quick suppers, easy to prepare if you're in a hurry, and one-pot dishes slow-cooked to maximize flavor. Remember that, although protein is an important part of any balanced diet, it's also important to choose lean cuts of meat and to make the most of the variety of fish and fowl available to vary your diet. Also, make sure you include lots of fresh vegetables and beans.

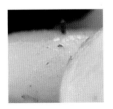   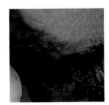  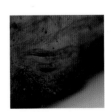

serves 4

Ginger-Marinated Salmon & Scallops

Ingredients

1 cup brown basmati rice

1/2 cucumber, diced

4 scallions, sliced

1/2 bunch fresh cilantro, chopped

1 red bell pepper, seeded and diced

1 fresh green chili, seeded and thinly sliced

juice of 1 lime

2 tbsp toasted sesame oil

1 lb 2 oz/500 g salmon fillet, skinned and cut into chunks

8 scallops, without corals, cleaned

1 3/4 oz/50 g fresh gingerroot

juice of 1 lemon

1 tbsp olive oil

green salad, to serve

Nutritional Fact

Salmon is high in essential fatty acids, which are good fats that help stabilize blood-sugar levels.

Serving Analysis

• Calories	559
• Protein	34g
• Carbohydrate	47g
• Sugars	3.1g
• Fat	26g
• Saturates	3.8g
• GI	Low

1 Bring a large pan of water to a boil, add the rice, and cook for 25 minutes, or until tender. Drain and let cool. Mix the cooled rice with the cucumber, scallions, cilantro, red bell pepper, chili, lime juice, and sesame oil in a bowl. Cover and set aside for the flavors to develop.

2 Meanwhile, put the salmon chunks into a shallow, nonmetallic bowl. Cut each scallop in half and add to the bowl. Using a garlic press or the back of a knife, crush the ginger to extract the juice. Mix the ginger juice with the lemon juice and olive oil in a small bowl or pitcher and pour over the seafood. Turn the seafood to coat in the marinade. Cover and let marinate in the refrigerator for 30 minutes. Soak 8 wooden skewers in cold water for 30 minutes, then drain.

3 Preheat the broiler to high. Thread an equal quantity of the salmon and scallops onto the skewers. Cook under the preheated broiler for 3–4 minutes on each side, or until cooked through.

4 Serve the hot seafood skewers with the rice salad and a green salad.

serves 4

Tuna & Avocado Salad

Ingredients

2 avocados, pitted, peeled, and cubed

9 oz/250 g cherry tomatoes, halved

2 red bell peppers, seeded and chopped

1 bunch fresh flatleaf parsley, chopped

2 garlic cloves, crushed

1 fresh red chili, seeded and finely chopped

juice of $1/2$ lemon

6 tbsp olive oil

pepper

3 tbsp sesame seeds

4 fresh tuna steaks, about $5^1/2$ oz/150 g each

8 cooked new potatoes, cubed

arugula leaves, to serve

1 Toss the avocados, tomatoes, red bell peppers, parsley, garlic, chili, lemon juice, and 2 tablespoons of the oil together in a large bowl. Season to taste with pepper, cover, and let chill in the refrigerator for 30 minutes.

2 Lightly crush the sesame seeds in a mortar with a pestle. Tip the crushed seeds onto a plate and spread out. Press each tuna steak in turn into the crushed seeds to coat on both sides.

3 Heat 2 tablespoons of the remaining oil in a skillet, add the potatoes, and cook, stirring frequently, for 5–8 minutes, or until crisp and brown. Remove from the skillet and drain on paper towels.

4 Wipe out the skillet, add the remaining oil, and heat over high heat until very hot. Add the tuna steaks and cook for 3–4 minutes on each side.

5 To serve, divide the avocado salad between 4 serving plates. Top each with a tuna steak, then sprinkle over the potatoes and a handful of arugula leaves.

Nutritional Fact

Avocados are rich in nutrients that can help to protect the eyes against diabetes-related damage.

Serving Analysis

• *Calories*	*785*
• *Protein*	*44g*
• *Carbohydrate*	*57g*
• *Sugars*	*7.1g*
• *Fat*	*46g*
• *Saturates*	*3g*
• *GI*	*Low*

serves 4

Sardines Escabechadas

Ingredients

2 lb 4 oz/1 kg fresh sardines, cleaned and scaled

2 tbsp all-purpose flour

generous 1/3 cup olive oil, plus 2 tbsp

1 large onion, sliced

2 garlic cloves, thinly sliced

1 small carrot, scraped and thinly sliced

2 tbsp chopped fresh parsley

1 tsp chopped fresh oregano

1 tsp ground cumin

pepper

1 tsp sugar

4 tbsp red wine vinegar

14 oz/400 g canned chopped tomatoes

generous 1 1/4 cups brown basmati rice

generous 3/4 cup chopped mixed fresh herbs

scant 1/2 cup chopped almonds

Nutritional Fact

Sardines provide beneficial fats, and onion and garlic help to balance blood sugar.

Serving Analysis

- Calories   1145
- Protein   56g
- Carbohydrate   66g
- Sugars   10.2g
- Fat   74.5g
- Saturates   8.7g
- GI   Medium

1 Preheat the oven to 325°F/160°C. Rinse the sardines and pat dry with paper towels. Spread the flour out on a plate. Roll each fish in the flour to coat.

2 Heat 1/4 cup of the oil in a large skillet over high heat, add the fish, in batches, and cook briefly on both sides until golden. Transfer to a large, shallow, ovenproof dish.

3 Heat the remaining oil (excluding the 2 tablespoons) in the skillet over medium heat, add the onion and garlic, and cook, stirring frequently, for 5 minutes, or until softened. Add the carrot and cook for an additional 5 minutes. Stir in the parsley, oregano, cumin, pepper to taste, sugar, vinegar, and tomatoes and let simmer for 15 minutes. Pour the sauce over the sardines and bake in the preheated oven for 15 minutes.

4 Meanwhile, bring a large pan of water to a boil, add the rice, and cook for 25 minutes, or until tender. Drain, transfer to a warmed serving dish, and mix with the herbs, almonds, the 2 tablespoons of oil, and pepper to taste. Serve the rice hot with the fish.

serves 4

Roast Beef Salad

Ingredients

1 lb 10 oz/750 g beef fillet, trimmed of any visible fat

pepper

2 tsp Worcestershire sauce

3 tbsp olive oil

14 oz/400 g green beans

3¹/₂ oz/100 g small pasta, such as orecchiette

2 red onions, finely sliced

1 large head radicchio

generous ¹/₄ cup green olives, pitted

scant ¹/₃ cup shelled hazelnuts, whole

For the dressing

1 tsp Dijon mustard

2 tbsp white wine vinegar

5 tbsp olive oil

Nutritional Fact
This recipe has a good mix of protein, fiber, beans, and onions, making it a good dish for stabilizing blood-sugar levels.

Serving Analysis
- *Calories*   748
- *Protein*   46g
- *Carbohydrate*   32g
- *Sugars*   7g
- *Fat*   51g
- *Saturates*   6g
- *GI*   Low

1 Preheat the oven to 425°F/220°C. Rub the beef with pepper to taste and Worcestershire sauce. Heat 2 tablespoons of the oil in a small roasting pan over high heat, add the beef, and sear on all sides. Transfer the dish to the preheated oven and roast for 30 minutes. Remove and let cool.

2 Bring a large pan of water to a boil, add the beans, and cook for 5 minutes, or until just tender. Remove with a slotted spoon and refresh the beans under cold running water. Drain and put into a large bowl.

3 Return the bean cooking water to a boil, add the pasta, and cook for 11 minutes, or until tender. Drain, return to the pan, and toss with the remaining oil.

4 Add the pasta to the beans with the onions, radicchio leaves, olives, and hazelnuts in a serving dish or salad bowl and arrange some thinly sliced beef on top.

5 Whisk the dressing ingredients together in a separate bowl, then pour over the salad and serve at once with extra sliced beef.

serves 4

Lamb with Rosemary, Potatoes, Peppers & Tomato

1 Preheat the oven to 350°F/180°C. Wipe the meat with paper towels and dust with the flour. Heat half the oil in an ovenproof casserole dish over medium heat. Add the meat, in batches, and brown on all sides. Remove from the casserole dish with a slotted spoon and keep warm.

2 Heat the remaining oil in the casserole dish over medium heat, add the onions and garlic, and cook, stirring frequently, for 5 minutes, or until lightly browned. Add the rosemary, then gradually add the stock, stirring constantly.

3 Return the meat to the casserole dish and add the potatoes, tomatoes, red bell peppers, orange rind, and pepper to taste. Bring up to a simmer, stirring constantly. Cover and cook in the preheated oven for 1 1/2 hours, stirring occasionally. Remove and discard the orange rind before serving.

Ingredients

2 lb/900 g lean lamb, cubed

1 tbsp all-purpose flour

2 tbsp olive oil

2 onions, sliced

2 garlic cloves, sliced

2 fresh rosemary sprigs

scant 2 1/2 cups lamb stock

8 small potatoes

9 oz/250 g cherry tomatoes

2 red bell peppers, seeded and sliced

2 pieces orange rind

pepper

Nutritional Fact

Lycopene, found in tomatoes and peppers, is an antioxidant that protects against damage from high insulin levels.

Serving Analysis

• *Calories*	*861*
• *Protein*	*46*
• *Carbohydrate*	*56g*
• *Sugars*	*7.8g*
• *Fat*	*50g*
• *Saturates*	*18.3g*
• *GI*	*Medium*

serves 4

Duck with Refried Beans, Olives & Thyme

Ingredients

4 duck breasts, skin on

3 garlic cloves, crushed

1 tbsp finely chopped fresh thyme

2 tbsp olive oil

1 lb 12 oz/800 g canned lima beans, drained and rinsed

12 black olives, pitted and sliced

pepper

arugula and watercress salad, to serve

Nutritional Fact

Garlic helps to lower blood pressure and cholesterol levels.

Serving Analysis

• Calories	497
• Protein	18g
• Carbohydrate	31g
• Sugars	1.6g
• Fat	38g
• Saturates	9.7g
• GI	Low

1 Wipe the duck breasts with paper towels and slash the skin across the breasts in several places. Rub half the garlic and the thyme into the cuts.

2 Heat the oil in a skillet over low heat, add the remaining garlic, and cook for 1 minute, stirring frequently. Add the beans and cook for 5 minutes. Add the olives and cook for an additional 5 minutes, or until the edges of the beans become golden and crusty. Season to taste with pepper.

3 Meanwhile, preheat the broiler to medium. Arrange the duck breasts, skin-side up, on the broiler pan. Cook under the preheated broiler for 5 minutes on each side for medium, or add an additional 3–5 minutes to the total cooking time for well done. Remove from the broiler and cut each breast into slices.

4 To serve, pile the beans onto 4 warmed serving plates and top with the sliced duck. Serve with an arugula and watercress salad.

serves 4

Roast Cinnamon Squab Chickens with Lentils

Ingredients

4 squab chickens, about
1 lb 2 oz/500 g each

2 tbsp maple syrup

1 tsp ground cinnamon

1 tbsp vegetable oil

generous ⅓ cup low-salt chicken
stock

2 red onions, sliced

1 tsp cumin seeds

1 tsp coriander seeds

1 tbsp olive oil

2 garlic cloves, crushed

1 lb 12 oz/800 g canned lentils,
drained and rinsed

1 tbsp unsalted butter

2 tbsp chopped fresh parsley

pepper

steamed broccoli or green beans,
to serve

1 Preheat the oven to 375°F/190°C. Arrange the squab chickens in a roasting pan. Mix the maple syrup, cinnamon, and vegetable oil together in a small bowl and brush over the breasts of the squab chickens. Pour the stock into the roasting pan and tuck the onion slices around the birds. Roast the squab chickens in the preheated oven for 35 minutes.

2 Meanwhile, heat a nonstick skillet over medium heat, add the cumin and coriander seeds, and cook, turning, until they start to give off an aroma. Tip into a mortar and finely crush with a pestle.

3 Heat the olive oil in a skillet over low heat, add the garlic and spices, and cook for 1–2 minutes, stirring constantly. Add the lentils and cook for 10–15 minutes, stirring occasionally.

4 When the birds are cooked, remove from the oven, transfer to a warmed plate, and keep warm. Put the roasting pan on the stove and bring the cooking juices up to a simmer. Stir in the butter and half the parsley. Season to taste with pepper.

5 To serve, divide the lentils between 4 warmed serving plates. Add a squab chicken to each plate, pour over the sauce, and sprinkle with the remaining parsley. Serve with steamed broccoli or green beans.

Nutritional Fact
One teaspoon of cinnamon a day has been proved useful for controlling Type II diabetes.

Serving Analysis

• Calories	769
• Protein	87g
• Carbohydrate	53g
• Sugars	13.4g
• Fat	23g
• Saturates	2.5g
• GI	Low

serves 4

Spanish Chicken with Preserved Lemons

Ingredients

Ingredients
1 tbsp all-purpose flour
4 chicken quarters, skin on
2 tbsp olive oil
2 garlic cloves, crushed
1 large Spanish onion, thinly sliced
3 cups low-salt chicken stock
$\frac{1}{2}$ tsp saffron threads
2 yellow bell peppers, seeded and cut into chunks
2 preserved lemons, cut into quarters
generous 1$\frac{1}{4}$ cups brown basmati rice
white pepper

12 pimiento-stuffed green olives

chopped fresh parsley, to garnish

green salad, to serve

Nutritional Fact

Although the lemons here are high in sugar, the chicken and basmati rice slow down sugar release into the bloodstream.

Serving Analysis

• Calories	547
• Protein	26g
• Carbohydrate	63g
• Sugars	5.7g
• Fat	22g
• Saturates	3.1g
• GI	Medium

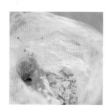  

1 Preheat the oven to 350°F/180°C. Put the flour into a large freezer bag. Add the chicken, close the top of the bag, and shake to coat with flour.

2 Heat the oil in a large skillet over low heat, add the garlic, and cook for 1 minute, stirring constantly.

3 Add the chicken to the skillet and cook over medium heat, turning frequently, for 5 minutes, or until the skin has lightly browned, then remove to a plate. Add the onion to the skillet and cook, stirring occasionally, for 10 minutes until soft.

4 Meanwhile, put the stock and saffron into a pan over low heat and heat through.

5 Transfer the chicken and onion to a large casserole dish, add the yellow bell peppers, lemons, and rice, then pour over the stock. Mix well and season to taste with pepper.

6 Cover and cook in the preheated oven for 50 minutes, or until the chicken is cooked through and tender. Reduce the oven temperature to 325°F/160°C. Add the olives to the casserole and cook for an additional 10 minutes.

7 Serve sprinkled with parsley and accompanied by a green salad.

Vegetarian

A revolution in vegetarian cooking means it is no longer considered the poor relation to cooking with meat or fish. Sophisticated ingredients drawn from a wide range of cuisines have made it now more popular than ever. A diet that contains plenty of vegetables will provide more fiber and more antioxidants and will usually be lower in fat. None of this means dull eating—as demonstrated by the recipes in this chapter.

serves 4

Celery Root, Chestnut, Spinach & Feta Phyllo Pies

Ingredients

4 tbsp olive oil

2 garlic cloves, crushed

$^1/_2$ large or 1 whole small head celery root, cut into short thin sticks

$5^5/_8$ cups baby spinach leaves

scant $^1/_2$ cup cooked, peeled chestnuts, coarsely chopped

7 oz/200 g feta cheese (drained weight), crumbled

1 egg

2 tbsp pesto sauce

1 tbsp finely chopped fresh parsley

pepper

4 sheets phyllo pastry, about 13 x 7 inches/32 x 18 cm each

green salad, to serve

1 Preheat the oven to 375°F/190°C. Heat 1 tablespoon of the oil in a large skillet over medium heat, add the garlic, and cook for 1 minute, stirring constantly. Add the celery root and cook for 5 minutes, or until soft and browned. Remove from the skillet and keep warm.

2 Add 1 tablespoon of the remaining oil to the skillet, then add the spinach, cover, and cook for 2–3 minutes, or until the spinach has wilted. Uncover and cook until any liquid has evaporated.

3 Mix the garlic and celery root, spinach, chestnuts, cheese, egg, pesto, parsley, and pepper to taste in a large bowl. Divide the mixture between 4 individual gratin dishes or put it all into 1 medium gratin dish.

4 Brush each sheet of phyllo with the remaining oil and arrange on top of the celery root mixture. Bake in the preheated oven for 15–20 minutes, or until browned. Serve at once with a green salad.

Nutritional Fact

Spinach contains lutein. This helps to prevent the eye degeneration that is associated with diabetes.

Serving Analysis

• Calories	545
• Protein	16g
• Carbohydrate	32g
• Sugars	5.7g
• Fat	40g
• Saturates	8.7g
• GI	Medium

serves 4

Roasted Garlic Sweet Potato, Broiled Eggplant & Bell Pepper Salad with Mozzarella

Ingredients

2 sweet potatoes, peeled and cut into chunks

2 tbsp olive oil

pepper

2 garlic cloves, crushed

1 large eggplant, sliced

2 red bell peppers, seeded and sliced

7 oz/200 g mixed salad greens

2 x 5¹/₂ oz/150 g mozzarella cheeses, drained and sliced

whole-wheat bread, to serve

For the dressing

1 tbsp balsamic vinegar

1 garlic clove, crushed

3 tbsp olive oil

1 small shallot, finely chopped

2 tbsp chopped mixed fresh herbs, such as tarragon, chervil, and basil

pepper

Nutritional Fact
Sweet potatoes contain betacarotene, which helps to protect the eyes, kidneys, and liver from damage.

Serving Analysis
- Calories   524
- Protein   22g
- Carbohydrate   34g
- Sugars   14.3g
- Fat   34g
- Saturates   0.1g
- GI   Medium

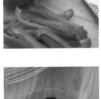

1 Preheat the oven to 375°F/190°C. Put the sweet potato chunks into a roasting pan with the oil, pepper to taste, and garlic and toss to combine. Roast in the preheated oven for 30 minutes, or until soft and slightly charred.

2 Meanwhile, preheat the broiler to high. Arrange the eggplant and bell pepper slices on the broiler pan and cook under the preheated broiler, turning occasionally, for 10 minutes, or until soft and slightly charred.

3 To make the dressing, whisk the vinegar, garlic, and oil together in a small bowl and stir in the shallot and herbs. Season to taste with pepper.

4 To serve, divide the salad greens between 4 serving plates and arrange the sweet potato, eggplant, bell peppers, and mozzarella on top. Drizzle with the dressing and serve with whole-wheat bread.

serves 4

Zucchini Fritters with Yogurt Dip

Ingredients

2–3 zucchini, about 14 oz/400 g

1 garlic clove, crushed

3 scallions, finely sliced

4½ oz/125 g feta cheese (drained weight), crumbled

2 tbsp finely chopped fresh parsley

2 tbsp finely chopped fresh mint

1 tbsp finely chopped fresh dill

½ tsp freshly grated nutmeg

2 tbsp all-purpose flour

pepper

2 eggs

2 tbsp olive oil

1 lemon, cut into quarters, to garnish

For the dip

scant 1¼ cups strained plain yogurt

¼ cucumber, diced

1 tbsp finely chopped fresh dill

pepper

Nutritional Fact

Eggs are one of the few vegetarian sources of protein that contain all the essential amino acids, which are the building blocks of protein.

Serving Analysis

- *Calories* — 266
- *Protein* — 13.3g
- *Carbohydrate* — 12.6g
- *Sugars* — 7g
- *Fat* — 18.5g
- *Saturates* — 6g
- *GI* — Medium

1 Grate the zucchini straight onto a clean dish towel and cover with another. Pat well and let stand for 10 minutes until the zucchini are dry.

2 Meanwhile, to make the dip, mix the yogurt, cucumber, dill, and pepper to taste in a serving bowl. Cover and let chill.

3 Tip the zucchini into a large bowl. Stir in the garlic, scallions, cheese, herbs, nutmeg, flour, and pepper to taste. Beat the eggs in a separate bowl and stir into the zucchini batter—the batter will be quite lumpy and uneven but this is fine.

4 Heat the oil in a large, wide pan over medium heat. Drop 4 tablespoonfuls of the batter into the skillet, with space in between, and cook for 2–3 minutes on each side. Remove, drain on paper towels, and keep warm. Cook the second batch of fritters in the same way. (There should be 8 fritters in total.)

5 Serve the fritters hot with the dip, garnished with lemon quarters.

serves 4

Mixed Mushroom Salad

Ingredients

3 tbsp pine nuts

2 red onions, cut into chunks

4 tbsp olive oil

2 garlic cloves, crushed

3 slices whole-wheat bread, cubed

7 oz/200 g mixed salad greens

9 oz/250 g cremini mushrooms, sliced

5¹/₂ oz/150 g shiitake mushrooms, sliced

5¹/₂ oz/150 g oyster mushrooms, torn

For the dressing

1 garlic clove, crushed

2 tbsp red wine vinegar

4 tbsp walnut oil

1 tbsp finely chopped fresh parsley

pepper

1 Preheat the oven to 350°F/180°C. Heat a nonstick skillet over medium heat, add the pine nuts, and cook, turning, until just browned. Tip into a bowl and set aside.

2 Put the onions and 1 tablespoon of the olive oil into a roasting pan and toss to coat. Roast in the preheated oven for 30 minutes.

3 Meanwhile, heat 1 tablespoon of the remaining oil with the garlic in the nonstick skillet over high heat. Add the bread and cook, turning frequently, for 5 minutes, or until brown and crisp. Remove from the skillet and set aside.

4 Divide the salad greens between 4 serving plates and add the roasted onions. To make the dressing, whisk the garlic, vinegar, and oil together in a small bowl. Stir in the parsley and season to taste with pepper. Drizzle over the salad and onions.

5 Heat the remaining oil in a skillet, add the cremini and shiitake mushrooms, and cook for 2–3 minutes, stirring frequently. Add the oyster mushrooms and cook for an additional 2–3 minutes. Divide the hot mushroom mixture between the 4 plates. Sprinkle over the pine nuts and croutons and serve.

Nutritional Fact

Pine nuts are a source of omega-6 oils that help control blood-sugar levels and regulate cholesterol.

Serving Analysis

• Calories	409
• Protein	8g
• Carbohydrate	27g
• Sugars	6.1g
• Fat	32.5g
• Saturates	2.7g
• GI	Low

serves 4

Baked Herb Ricotta

Ingredients

1 tbsp olive oil, plus extra for drizzling
2 lb 4 oz/1 kg fresh ricotta cheese, drained
3 eggs, lightly beaten
3 tbsp chopped fresh herbs, such as tarragon, parsley, dill, and chives
pepper
1/2 tsp paprika, plus extra for sprinkling
4 slices whole-wheat bread
green salad, to serve

1 Preheat the oven to 350°F/180°C. Brush a 2-lb 4 oz/1-kg nonstick loaf pan with the oil.

2 Put the ricotta into a bowl and beat well. Add the eggs and stir until smooth, then stir in the herbs, pepper to taste, and paprika.

3 Spoon the mixture into the prepared pan and put into a roasting pan half-filled with water. Bake in the preheated oven for 30–40 minutes, or until set. Remove from the oven and let cool.

4 Meanwhile, cut the crusts off the bread to make Melba toast. Cut each slice widthwise in half to create 2 thin slices. Cut each half diagonally into triangles. Arrange in a single layer on a baking sheet and bake in the oven for 10 minutes.

5 Turn the baked ricotta out onto a serving dish, drizzle with a little oil, and sprinkle with paprika. Serve with the Melba toast and a green salad.

Nutritional Fact

This dish is very low in GI values, and so helps to stabilize blood-sugar levels, as well as providing good levels of protein.

Serving Analysis

• Calories	399
• Protein	29g
• Carbohydrate	13g
• Sugars	1.5g
• Fat	26g
• Saturates	1.4g
• GI	Low

serves 4

Chili Bean Cakes with Avocado Salsa

Ingredients

$^3/_8$ cup pine nuts

15 oz/425 g canned mixed beans, drained and rinsed

$^1/_2$ red onion, finely chopped

1 tbsp tomato paste

$^1/_2$ fresh red chili, seeded and finely chopped

1 cup fresh brown bread crumbs

1 egg, beaten

1 tbsp finely chopped fresh cilantro

2 tbsp corn oil

1 lime, cut into quarters, to garnish

4 toasted whole-wheat bread rolls, to serve (optional)

For the salsa

1 avocado, pitted, peeled, and chopped

$3^1/_2$ oz/100 g tomatoes, seeded and chopped

2 garlic cloves, crushed

2 tbsp finely chopped fresh cilantro

1 tbsp olive oil

pepper

juice of $^1/_2$ lime

1 Heat a nonstick skillet over medium heat, add the pine nuts, and cook, turning, until just browned. Tip into a bowl and set aside.

2 Put the beans into a large bowl and coarsely mash. Add the onion, tomato paste, chili, pine nuts, and half the bread crumbs and mix well. Add half the egg and the cilantro and mash together, adding a little more egg, if needed, to bind the mixture.

3 Form the mixture into 4 flat cakes. Coat with the remaining bread crumbs, cover, and let chill in the refrigerator for 30 minutes.

4 To make the salsa, mix all the ingredients together in a serving bowl, cover, and let chill in the refrigerator until required.

5 Heat the oil in a skillet over medium heat, add the bean cakes, and cook for 4–5 minutes on each side, or until crisp and heated through. Remove from the skillet and drain on paper towels.

6 Serve each bean cake in a toasted whole-wheat roll, if desired, with the salsa, garnished with a lime quarter.

Nutritional Fact

Avocados are high in beneficial fats; garlic and beans help control blood-sugar levels.

Serving Analysis

• Calories	404
• Protein	13.4g
• Carbohydrate	31g
• Sugars	4.8g
• Fat	27.5g
• Saturates	3.8g
• GI	Low

serves 4

Warm Red Lentil Salad with Goat Cheese

Ingredients

2 tbsp olive oil	1 tsp hazelnut oil
2 tsp cumin seeds	5 1/2 oz/150 g soft goat cheese
2 garlic cloves, crushed	4 tbsp strained plain yogurt
2 tsp grated fresh gingerroot	pepper
1 1/2 cups split red lentils	1 lemon, cut into quarters, to garnish
3 cups vegetable stock	toasted rye bread, to serve
2 tbsp chopped fresh mint	
2 tbsp chopped fresh cilantro	
2 red onions, thinly sliced	
4 3/8 cups baby spinach leaves	

Nutritional Fact

Lentils and spinach contain B vitamins and iron. These are important for energy production and controlling sugar cravings.

Serving Analysis

• Calories	310
• Protein	16g
• Carbohydrate	24g
• Sugars	6g
• Fat	17g
• Saturates	5.9g
• GI	Low

1 Heat half the olive oil in a large pan over medium heat, add the cumin seeds, garlic, and ginger and cook for 2 minutes, stirring constantly.

2 Stir in the lentils, then add the stock, a ladleful at a time, until it is all absorbed, stirring constantly—this will take about 20 minutes. Remove from the heat and stir in the herbs.

3 Meanwhile, heat the remaining olive oil in a skillet over medium heat, add the onions, and cook, stirring frequently, for 10 minutes, or until soft and lightly browned.

4 Toss the spinach in the hazelnut oil in a bowl, then divide between 4 serving plates.

5 Mash the goat cheese with the yogurt in a small bowl and season to taste with pepper.

6 Divide the lentils between the serving plates and top with the onions and goat cheese mixture. Garnish with lemon quarters and serve with toasted rye bread.

serves 4

Vegetable Brochettes with Jerusalem Artichoke Hummus

Ingredients

8 shallots, peeled

8 white mushrooms

2 yellow zucchini, cut into rounds

2 red bell peppers, seeded and cut into chunks

1 small eggplant, cut into chunks

1 sweet potato, peeled and cut into chunks

2 tbsp olive oil

juice of 1 lemon

1 fresh rosemary sprig, leaves removed and finely chopped

toasted whole-wheat bread, rubbed with a halved garlic clove, to serve

For the hummus

12 oz/350 g Jerusalem artichokes

1 tbsp olive oil

1 tbsp butter

³/₄ cup milk

generous 3¹/₄ cups cooked chickpeas, or canned ones, drained and rinsed

1 tsp ground cumin

2 tbsp lemon juice

1 garlic clove, crushed

pepper

1 Presoak 8 wooden skewers in cold water for 30 minutes, then drain. Thread an equal quantity of the vegetables onto the skewers and put into a shallow, nonmetallic dish. Mix the oil, lemon juice, and rosemary together in a small bowl and pour over the skewers. Cover and let marinate at room temperature for 30 minutes.

2 Meanwhile, to make the hummus, put the artichokes into a large pan of boiling water and cook for 5 minutes, or until tender. Drain, transfer the artichokes to a food processor or blender with the oil, butter, and milk and process until smooth. Add the chickpeas, cumin, lemon juice, garlic, and pepper to taste and process again until smooth. Transfer to a serving dish.

3 Preheat the broiler to medium. Lift the brochettes from the marinade, arrange on the broiler pan and cook under the preheated broiler for 15 minutes, turning frequently, until the vegetables are soft and flecked with brown.

4 Serve the brochettes at once with the hummus and toasted whole-wheat bread rubbed with garlic.

Nutritional Fact

Jerusalem artichokes contain inulin, a natural fructose that can help to lower insulin levels.

Serving Analysis
- Calories   413
- Protein   11g
- Carbohydrate   60g
- Sugars   17.4g
- Fat   16.6g
- Saturates   3g
- GI   Medium

Desserts & Baking

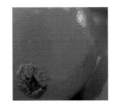

A wide range of candies and desserts can be eaten by people with diabetes, as long as the right ingredients are used. Fruit desserts are particularly good, while sherbets, and frozen desserts made with lowfat yogurt are also suitable. Vary the combinations and make use of the wide selection of exotic fruits now available to enjoy delicious healthy desserts.

serves 4

Blueberry Frozen Yogurt

 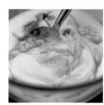 

Ingredients

³/₄ cup fresh blueberries

finely grated rind and juice of 1 orange

3 tbsp maple syrup

1 lb 2 oz/500 g plain lowfat yogurt

Nutritional Fact
Blueberries may increase sensitivity to insulin and help to control Type II diabetes.

Serving Analysis

• Calories	157
• Protein	7g
• Carbohydrate	29g
• Sugars	26g
• Fat	2g
• Saturates	1.1g
• GI	Low

1 Put the blueberries and orange juice into a food processor or blender and process to a purée. Strain through a nylon strainer into a bowl or pitcher.

2 Stir the maple syrup and yogurt together in a large mixing bowl, then fold in the fruit purée.

3 Churn the mixture in an ice-cream machine, following the manufacturer's instructions, then freeze for 5–6 hours. If you don't have an ice-cream machine, transfer the mixture to a freezerproof container, and freeze for 2 hours. Remove from the freezer, turn out into a bowl, and beat until smooth. Return to the freezer and freeze until firm.

serves 4

Peach & Ginger Dessert

Ingredients

14 oz/400 g ripe peaches

1 tsp chopped preserved ginger in syrup

1 lb 2 oz/500 g plain lowfat yogurt

3 tbsp ginger syrup from the preserved ginger

4 amaretti cookies, crushed

Nutritional Fact
Peaches have a low GI score, and ginger lowers cholesterol and improves circulation.

Serving Analysis

- Calories   300
- Protein   11g
- Carbohydrate   37g
- Sugars   32.5g
- Fat   6.7g
- Saturates   1.5g
- GI   Medium

1 Put the peaches into a large, heatproof bowl and cover with boiling water. Let stand for 1 minute. Using a slotted spoon, lift out the fruit. When cool enough to handle, peel away the skins, remove and discard the pits, and coarsely chop the flesh. Transfer to a food processor or blender, add the ginger, and process to a purée.

2 Stir the yogurt and ginger syrup together in a bowl.

3 Spoon a little of the yogurt mixture into 4 serving glasses, then top with a spoonful of the fruit purée. Repeat until the mixtures are used up. Let chill in the refrigerator for 3 hours.

4 Sprinkle over the crushed amaretti cookies before serving.

serves 4

Summer Fruit Elderberry Flower Jelly

Ingredients

4 leaves gelatin

generous ¹/₄ cup boiling water

2 tbsp elderberry flower cordial

³/₄ cup cold water

⁷/₈ cup mixed berries, such as raspberries, red currants, and blackberries

4 tsp light cream

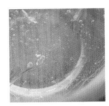  

Nutritional Fact
Berries in general provide certain plant chemicals. These give them their colors and help to balance blood sugar.

Serving Analysis

• Calories	67
• Protein	6.7g
• Carbohydrate	9.6g
• Sugars	4.9g
• Fat	0.5g
• Saturates	0.2g
• GI	Low

1 Soak the gelatin leaves in a bowl of cold water for 10 minutes. Lift out and squeeze gently, then mix with the boiling water in a heatproof bowl. Stir until the gelatin has completely dissolved.

2 Stir in the elderberry flower cordial and cold water.

3 Divide the berries between 4 wine glasses and pour over the elderberry flower mixture. Let chill in the refrigerator for 3 hours.

4 Serve each jelly with a spoonful of cream.

serves 4

Broiled Honeyed Figs with Sabayon

Ingredients

8 fresh figs, cut in half

4 tbsp honey

2 fresh rosemary sprigs, leaves removed and finely chopped (optional)

3 eggs

1 Preheat the broiler to high. Arrange the figs, cut-side up, on the broiler pan. Brush with half the honey and sprinkle over the rosemary, if using.

2 Cook under the preheated broiler for 5–6 minutes, or until just starting to caramelize.

3 Meanwhile, to make the sabayon, in a large, heatproof bowl, lightly whisk the eggs with the remaining honey, then place over a pan of simmering water. Using a hand-held electric whisk, beat the eggs and honey together for 10 minutes, or until pale and thick.

4 Put 4 fig halves on each of 4 serving plates, add a generous spoonful of the sabayon, and serve at once.

Nutritional Fact

Fresh figs release their sugars much more slowly than dried ones. They contain minerals that can help with insulin sensitivity.

Serving Analysis

- *Calories* — 190
- *Protein* — 5.4g
- *Carbohydrate* — 36g
- *Sugars* — 32g
- *Fat* — 4g
- *Saturates* — 1.2g
- *GI* — Medium

serves 4

Little Semisweet Chocolate Mousse Pots with Poached Berries

Nutritional Fact
Semisweet chocolate is lower in sugar than milk chocolate and can be an occasional treat if eaten in small amounts, such as in this recipe.

Serving Analysis
* Calories   241
* Protein   4.4g
* Carbohydrate   24g
* Sugars   20g
* Fat   16g
* Saturates   8.7g
* GI   Medium

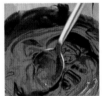

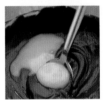

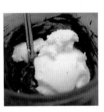

Ingredients

3¹/₂ oz/100 g semisweet chocolate, minimum 70% cocoa solids

2 tbsp unsalted butter

2 eggs, separated

1 tbsp maple syrup

scant ¹/₂ cup mixed dark berries, such as blackberries, black currants, and blueberries

1 tbsp crème de cassis

fresh mint leaves, to decorate

1 Break the chocolate into pieces, put into a heatproof bowl with the butter, and place over a pan of simmering water. Let melt, then let cool slightly. Stir in the egg yolks and maple syrup.

2 Whisk the egg whites in a large bowl until stiff, then fold into the cooled chocolate mixture. Divide between 4 ramekins and let chill in the refrigerator for 3 hours.

3 Meanwhile, put the berries into a small pan with the crème de cassis over low heat, and cook for 5–10 minutes, or until the berries are glossy and soft. Let cool.

4 To serve, spoon the berries on top of the chocolate mousse and decorate with mint leaves.

makes 16

Nutty Granola Squares

Ingredients

4 oz/115 g unsalted butter, plus extra for greasing

4 tbsp honey

$^1/_8$ cup unrefined superfine sugar

scant 3 cups rolled oats

generous $^1/_8$ cup dried cranberries

generous $^1/_8$ cup pitted dates, chopped

generous $^1/_8$ cup hazelnuts, chopped

$^5/_8$ cup slivered almonds

1 Preheat the oven to 375°F/190°C. Grease an 8-inch/20-cm square baking pan.

2 Melt the butter with the honey and sugar in a pan and stir together. Add the remaining ingredients and mix thoroughly.

3 Turn the mixture into the prepared pan and press down well. Bake in the preheated oven for 20–30 minutes.

4 Remove from the oven and let cool in the pan. Cut into 16 squares.

Nutritional Fact

Oats and nuts ensure the slow release of sugars and are, therefore, good sources of energy, which can help to alleviate sugar cravings.

Serving Analysis
- *Calories*   167
- *Protein*   3.3g
- *Carbohydrate*   17g
- *Sugars*   6.9g
- *Fat*   10g
- *Saturates*   4g
- *GI*   *Medium*

serves 4

Walnut & Pecan Soda Bread

Nutritional Fact
Walnuts are a very good source of omega-3 and -6 oils, which help to balance blood sugar.

Serving Analysis
- *Calories*   *613*
- *Protein*   *17g*
- *Carbohydrate*   *94g*
- *Sugars*   *7.2g*
- *Fat*   *19g*
- *Saturates*   *2.1g*
- *GI*   *Medium*

Ingredients

1 lb/450 g all-purpose flour, plus extra for flouring

1 tsp baking soda

1 tsp cream of tartar

1 tsp salt

1 tsp sugar

generous ³⁄₈ cup chopped walnuts

scant ¹⁄₂ cup chopped pecans

1¹⁄₄ cups buttermilk

1 Preheat the oven to 350°F/180°C. Dust a baking sheet with flour.

2 Sift the flour, baking soda, cream of tartar, and salt into a large mixing bowl. Stir in the sugar and nuts. Pour in the buttermilk and mix to a soft dough.

3 With floured hands, knead the dough briefly on a lightly floured counter, then shape into a circle 8–10 inches/20–25 cm in diameter and transfer to the prepared baking sheet. Cut a cross in the top of the dough.

4 Bake in the preheated oven for 30 minutes, then cover with foil and bake for an additional 15 minutes.

5 Remove from the oven and let cool slightly. Serve warm in slices.